**최원철 시집**
The Collection of Won Chul Choi's Poems

**한영대역판**
*Korean-English Edition*

# 산에도 들국화가 있더라

(Chrysanthemums in the Mountain)

우전雨田 최 원 철
Won Chul Choi, Dr. rer. nat.
(Pseudonym : Rain-Blessed Field)

The Collection of Won Chul Choi's Poems
최원철 시집

*Korean-English Edition*
한영대역판

# Chrysanthemums in the Mountain
산에도 들국화가 있더라

Won Chul Choi, Dr. rer. nat.
(Pseudonym : Rain-Blessed Field)
우전雨田 최 원 철

도서출판
Doosoncomm Publishing Co. Book

|저자소개|

저자 최원철은 현재, 시인 및 수필가로써 한국펜클럽한국본부 이사 및 부산문인협회 이사이다. 그리고 현재 부산대학교 명예교수로 있다.

시집으로는
① 『그리움이 진하여 눈물이 될 때』 (제1집)
② 『기막힌 일 당하거든』 (제2집)
③ 『비오는 날 누구와 만나도 사랑하게 된다』 (제3집)
④ 『널 그리며』 (제4집)
⑤ 『피안의 섬』 (제5집) ― 문예시대 작가상 수상
⑥ 『어느 고목의 독백』 (제6집, 한영대역)
  ― 2010년 5월 19일 제27차 영광문학 토론회
⑦ 『깍지 속 콩순이』 (제7집, 한영대역)
⑧ 『엄마, 나 이제 그만 울까요?』 (제8집, 한영대역)
⑨ 『산에도 들국화가 있더라』 (제9집, 한영대역)

| About the Author |

The author, Dr. Won Chul Choi, is currently a poet and essayist and is the former director of the Korea Division of the International Pen Club, the director of the Busan Writers Association. And author is currently an emeritus professor at Pusan National University.

The author's poem collections that have been published so far include
① When Longing Grows Strong Enough to Become Tears (collection 1)
② If an Awful Thing Happens to You (collection 2)
③ Rainy Days Make Me Love Anybody I Meet (collection 3)
④ Missing You (collection 4)
⑤ An Island of Nirvana (collection 5) - was awarded a writer's prize by the Age of Literary Arts
⑥ Monologue of an aged Tree (collection 6, Korean-English edition)
　- The 27th Yeonggwang Literature Forum, May 19, 2010
⑦ Maiden Beans in a Bean Pod (collection 7, Korean-English edition)
⑧ Mother, Should I Stop Crying Now? (collection 8, Korean-English edition)
⑨ Chrysanthemums in the Mountain (collection 9, Korean-English edition)

| 서 문 |

　인간은 자연이라는 환경을 떠나 살 수가 없습니다. 그 속에서 사고思考하고, 사랑하며 살고 있습니다. 계절이 바뀔 때마다 아름다움도 바뀌어 가고 있습니다.

　아무리 여유가 없는 생활이요 각박한 생활이라도 우리는 바람에 흔들리는 나뭇잎을 볼 줄 알아야 하겠고, 하늘에 떠 있는 뭉게구름도 볼 줄 알아야 할 것입니다. 그 속에는 삶의 진실이 있고 사랑이 있기 때문입니다. 또한, 슬픔도 있습니다.

　요즘 녹색산업이 발달하기 시작함에 따라, 인간의 감성이 문학으로 표출 하지 않을 수 없습니다. 그래서 산림문학(녹색문학)의 장이 열려지고 탄생한 것으로 알고 있습니다. 좀 더 눈을 돌려보면 산과 들에 있는 나무가 우리에게 주는 혜택은 일일이 밝히지 않아도 너무나 많을 것입니다.

　우리 주위에는 많은 숲들이 있습니다. 거기에서 일어나는 이야기를 우리의 인생의 삶과 연결시키고 싶었습니다. 그래서 이 책의 제목을 "산에도 들국화가 있더라"로 하고 그 내용은 제1장에서 '숲 속 이야기'를, 제2장에서는 '자연의 숨소리'로 나누어 글을 써보았습니다.

| Preface |

Humans cannot live apart from the natural environment. They think, love and live in this environment. Beauty changes just as the seasons change.

No matter how busy and tiresome life is, we should know how to look at the leaves rustling in the wind, and the clouds in the sky. This is because within it is the truth of life and love. There is also sadness.

With the recent development of green industries, we have no choice but to express human sentiment through literature. That is why the doors to The Forest Literature(Green literature) have opened. I won't have to mention how many benefits the mountains and trees give us just by looking around us.

There are many forests surrounding us. I wanted to connect the stories from there with our lives. That is why I entitled this book, "Chrysanthemums in the Mountain". Chapter 1 is 'Forest Story', and Chapter 2 is 'Breath of Nature'.

자연 과학을 연구한 한 사람으로서 자연과의 대화를 엮어 보는 단편의 시집도 뜻있는 일이라 생각해 봅니다. 물론 시적 표현이 서툴지는 몰라도, 많은 독자들께서 격려와 지도 편달의 마음을 가져 주시면 대단히 감사하겠습니다.

2013. 6.


자연 속에서 나를 발견하려는 어느 아침에

최 원 철

As a person who studied natural sciences, I believe that it is meaningful to publish a book of poems dealing with dialogues with nature. Though I may be lacking in poetic expression, I would like to ask for the encouragement and criticism of many readers. Thank you.

June, 2013

On a morning day that I discover myself in nature,

Won Chul Choi

| 차례 |

저자소개 _ 4
서문 _ 6

## 제1장 숲 속 이야기

산에도 들국화가 있더라 _ 18
잎의 몽상夢想 _ 22
하얀 민들레 _ 26
복수초福壽草 _ 30
넝쿨 _ 32
달맞이꽃 _ 34
나이테 _ 36
어느 곰팡이의 서식棲息 _ 38
양파 _ 40
갈대 소리 _ 44
은행잎 _ 46
배추의 귀 _ 48
동구 밖 정자나무 _ 52
해바라기 _ 56
꽃가루의 꿈 _ 60
꽃가루 알레르기 _ 62
숟가락으로 퍼먹는 들판 _ 66
뻐꾸기 _ 70
매미 _ 72

| Contents |

About the Author _ 5
Preface _ 7

## Chapter 1 Forest Story

Chrysanthemums in the Mountain _ 19
Dream Vision of a Leaf _ 23
White Dandelion _ 27
An Adonis Flower _ 31
Vines _ 33
Evening Primrose _ 35
Tree Rings _ 37
Habitat of a Mold _ 39
Onion _ 41
Sound of Reeds _ 45
Ginkgo Leaves _ 47
Ears of Chinese Cabbage _ 49
A Shade Tree at the Outskirts of the Village _ 53
Sunflower _ 57
Dream of Pollen _ 61
Pollen Allergy _ 63
Scooping a Field with a Spoon _ 67
Cuckoo _ 71
Cicada _ 73

| 차례 |

진딧물 _ 74
누에 _ 76
달팽이 _ 78
공벌레 _ 80
무당벌레 _ 82
칠성무당벌레 _ 84
좀벌레 _ 86
나방이 _ 90
맹꽁이 사랑 _ 92
공생共生 _ 96


## 제2장 자연의 숨소리

가야산 기슭에서 _ 100
잃어버린 시간을 찾아 _ 104
교신交信 _ 108
달의 소묘素描 _ 112
상현上弦달 _ 116
달빛 _ 120
메마른 계곡 _ 124
눈물이 흘러내린 계곡 _ 126

| Contents |

Aphid _ *75*
Silkworm _ *77*
Snail _ *79*
Pill Bug _ *81*
Ladybug _ *83*
Seven-spotted Ladybug _ *85*
Silverfish _ *87*
Moth _ *91*
Narrow-Mouthed Toad's Love _ *93*
Symbiosis _ *97*

## Chapter 2  Breath of Nature

At the Foot of Gayasan(Mt.) _ *101*
In Search of Lost Time _ *105*
Contact _ *109*
Drawing of the Moon _ *113*
Young Moon _ *117*
Moonlight _ *121*
Dry Valley _ *125*
Valley of Tears _ *127*

| 차례 |

잊지 못해 _ 128
돈 _ 130
언덕 _ 132
만우절萬愚節 _ 136
소금 기둥 _ 138
해변을 걸으며 _ 140
소나기 지난 후 _ 142
태종대 _ 146
나이아가라 폭포에서 _ 150
몽돌 _ 154
이기대 산책 _ 156
낙원의 끄트머리에서 _ 158
징검다리 _ 162
자연自然의 신음呻吟 _ 164
바람 부는 날 _ 168
신神이 쓴 책 _ 170
통영의 항구에서 _ 174

| Contents |

Unforgettable _ *129*
Money _ *131*
Hill _ *133*
April Fool's Day _ *137*
Salt Pillar _ *139*
Walking along the Seashore _ *141*
After the Shower _ *143*
Taejongdae _ *147*
Niagara Falls _ *151*
A Round Rock _ *155*
Walking at Yigidae _ *157*
At the End of Paradise _ *159*
Stepping Stones _ *163*
Groaning of Nature _ *165*
A Windy Day _ *169*
A Book by God _ *171*
At Tongyoung Harbor _ *175*

제1장

숲 속 이야기

Chapter 1

Forest Story

# 산에도 들국화가 있더라

검은 구름 자욱한 장자산*을 내려오다
단풍나무 아래서 파르르 떨고 있는 들국화를 만났다.
가을의 향내를 맡고 싶어 말을 건넸다
스산한 바람이 곁에 있는 억새풀을 흔들어 고요를 깨우고
한 줄기 새어나온 햇빛은 꽃잎 위에 하늘을 새긴다.

들이나 광야에서 뿌리를 내려 한 곳에만 사는 줄 알았는데
산에도 들국화가 있더라.

많은 사람들이 지나가는 숲길에서
애처롭게 서 있는 들국화 한 송이
퇴행성관절염으로 더 오르지 못하고 산허리에 앉아서
그리운 님의 발자국소리 들으려 쉬고 있는 들국화
벌써 무서리 내리려 하늘은 차다
더 이상 나는 위로의 언어를 잊어버렸다.

## Chrysanthemums in the Mountain

Climbing down from Jangjasan* blanketed by dark clouds, I see a chrysanthemum under a maple tree fluttering.
Hoping to smell the scent of autumn, I spoke to it,
Bleak winds shake the silver grass to stir the silence,
And a ray of sunlight engraves the heavens on a flower petal.

I thought that they only took root and lived in fields or plains, but there were also chrysanthemums in the mountains.

In a forest path passed by many people,
there is a lonely chrysanthemum standing alone.
Unable to climb beyond the hillside because of degenerative arthritis,
the chrysanthemum rests while listening to the footsteps of whom it longs for,
but the early frost has already come and the skies are frigid.
From here, I forget my comforting language.

추억이 많을수록 그리움이 크기에
이렇게 높이 올라
내님이 오시려나 바라보는 붉은 저녁놀.
서러운 그리움을 이기지 못해
산에도 들국화가 피었나보다.

*장자산: 부산 남구 용호동에 위치한 장자산의 명칭은 장산봉(長山峰)이 원래의 이름이었지만 봉(峰)을 산으로 격상시켜 장자산(長子山)으로 불렀고 이기대를 포함하여 아름다운 곳이다.

(2013년 4월 27일)

As longing grows with more memories,
it climbed this high
and stared down to see when its love will come - the evening sunset.
Unable to defeat its sad longing,
that is why the chrysanthemum bloomed in the mountain.

\* Jangjasan: The original name of Jangjasan (Mt.) located in Yongho-dong, Nam-gu, Busan was Jangsanbong (peak), but *bong* (peak) was raised to *san* (mountain), and it is a beautiful place together with Igidae.

(April 27, 2013)

# 잎의 몽상夢想

푸른 잎 속에 태양이 머문다.
엽록체 속에 숨겨져 있는
그라나와 스트로마를 깨운다.
그대가 싫든 좋든 간에
욕정欲情의 사과를 익게 한다.

이슬내리는 밤이나, 그리움에 설레는 밤이거나
별들은 하루가 천년,
천년이 하루가 되는 신神의 계산법으로
수억 광년을 타고 고요 속에서만
그대의 스트로마에 내린다.
역사가 이루어진다.
그대 깊숙이 간직한 스트로마가 밤이기 때문이다.

아직 태양이 잎에 머물고 있기에
연명延命해야 할 산소酸素를 만들고 있다
사랑으로 위장된 그라나를 통해
끊임없이 나눔의 행사처럼 번져 갈
그리움으로,
고독으로,
욕망慾望으로……

# Dream Vision of a Leaf

In the green leaf stays the sun.
Hidden inside the chloroplast,
grana and stroma are awakened.
Whether you like it or not,
it ripens the fruit of desire.

Whether on a drizzling night or a night excited with longing,
a day is a thousand years for stars,
and a thousand years is a day in the eyes of the god,
and after millions of light years, only in silence,
it stops at your stroma.
History is made.
Because the stroma deep within you becomes the night.

Because the sun still lingers in the leaf,
oxygen needed for life is created.
Through the grana under the disguise of love,
like a festival of ceaseless sharing
to longing,
to loneliness,
to despair…….

*그라나: 엽록체에서 광합성으로 산소를 합성하는 곳
*스트로마: 엽록체의 기질을 말함(탄수화물을 합성하는 곳)

(2011년 5월 3일)

*Grana: where oxygen is made through photosynthesis in chloroplast
*Stroma: refers to the texture of chloroplast (where carbohydrates are made)


(May 3, 2011)

## 하얀 민들레

나의 정원에 심은 흰 민들레 한 그루
땅속 깊이 다년생 뿌리를 내렸네.
거름을 주어 옥토를 만들고
추위에 떨 때는 바람막이로 가리고
메마른 날에는 물을 주었네.
여름이 오고 또 여름이 세 번이나 올 동안 바람이 불어도 흔들리지 않고
순결한 호흡으로 하얗게 피우는 꽃잎에서 내 영혼은 편히 쉬었네.

잎이 자라 무성하여 꽃대가 올라와
철마다 변하는 하늘의 색깔을 배우고 자유의 나래를 폈네.
행여나 구름 속에 황홀한 꿈이 있을까
영글어진 혜안慧眼의 씨앗에 방랑의 유전자를 싣고 구름 위로 날아가 버렸네.

# White Dandelion

A white dandelion planted in my garden,
it placed its perennial roots deep inside the soil.
Fertilized to enrich the soil,
and sheltered from the wind when cold,
I gave it water on dry days.
Even after three summers came and went, it shivers not in the wind
and its white flower that breathes innocence gives refuge to my soul.

Its leaves grow and the flower stalk becomes erect,
and learns the seasonally changing colors of the skies and spreads its wings of freedom.
Imagining that there may be a fantastic dream inside the clouds,
it places genes of wandering in the seed of ripened insight, and flies far above the clouds.

텅 빈 머리만 올려놓은 줄기는 메마르고 재생의 능력마저 잃어버린 뿌리
집 나간 사랑은 내가 머물던 자리를 비켜가 또 다른 땅에서 뿌리내리는 하얀 민들레

진실한 사랑을 앗아간 꽃송이는 누구의 소유도 될 수 없음을 몰랐던 우둔한 머리에는 통증만 가득하네.

(2013년 4월 21일)

The stem with a bald head is a root that is dry, having lost its ability to reproduce,

a love that has left also avoids where I am and is a white dandelion that finds another land to place its roots.

The flower that took away true love only leaves pain in a dull head that did not know that love cannot be possessed by anyone.

(April 21, 2013)

## 복수초福壽草

그대 너무 멀리 떨어져 볼 수가 없어
봄의 향기 타고 가 그대 앞에 내려
노란 복수초 꽃으로 피고 싶어라

아무도 밟지 못한 하얀 눈길 위에
차가운 바람이 세차게 불어와도
제일 먼저 피어나 그대 맞으리라.

부드러운 두 손으로 나를 감쌀 때
노란 꽃잎 한 잎 한 잎 새겨진 사랑
그대 품에 고요히 안기고 싶어라

현란하게 채색된 저녁노을에
고뇌로 버무려진 세월을 지나
나, 그대 품속에서 쉬고 싶어라

(2013년 3월 13일)

# An Adonis Flower

You are too far away that I cannot see you,
I want to be brought in front of you with the scent of spring,
and bloom as a yellow adonis flower.

On a clear white path of snow,
even if the cold winds blow angrily,
I want to bloom first to greet you.

When caressing me with your two soft hands,
love engraved in each of the yellow petals,
Oh, how I wish to rest silently in your embrace.

In the brilliantly colored evening sunset,
passing the days spotted with anguish,
I wish to rest in your bosom.

(March 13, 2013)

# 넝쿨

혼미한 세월의 숲 속에서 생존경쟁이 처절하다. 뿌리가 아닐 바에야 위로 자라야 한다.
실용의 가치가 끝나면 더 나은 자를 찾는,
비교의 원리를 철저히 따르는 변성變性된 사랑의 습성.
남의 목을 조이고 밟고 일어서야 살 수 있는 처절한 운명.
좌절을 바탕으로 성공하려는 비운의 삶을 살아야 한다.

비바람에 흔들리며 날마다 커가는 푸른 잎.
햇볕 쨍쨍 내리쬐어 숨이 턱까지 차오르는 무더운 길가에 사랑했던 사람을 팽개쳐버리고 혼자 차를 몰고 가버리는 악몽이 되살아난다면, 감정만 따라가며 살아야 하는 근성이 자연으로부터 물려받은 DNA의 무서운 저주일까, 혼자 살아남을 축복일까.

이곳 저곳,
시련의 숲에서 빛을 향하여 타오르는 노래
'햇빛을 보아야 살아요.'

휘감아 오르는 몸짓은
수줍은 열정의 간절한 기도

(2013년 3월 11일)

# Vines

Survival is fierce in the forest of chaotic time. If it is not a root, it must grow up.

If it's of practical value, a better one is sought after,

the nature of love that changes its nature according to the principle of comparison.

The gruesome destiny in which one can live only by strangling and standing on top of others.

They must live star-crossed lives for success, based on failure.

The green leaf grows by the day amidst rustling winds.

The nightmare of abandoning a loved one and driving away alone on a sunny and hot day, is the dire curse of DNA received from nature in which one must live according to emotions. Or is it a blessing of being able to live alone?

Here and there,
a song burns from the forest of despair, to light,
'Living in the face of the sun'.

The twisting body
is a desperate prayer of bashful passion.

(March 11, 2013)

# 달맞이꽃

　어둠 속에서 욕망의 불꽃을 태우는 꽃들이 즐비한 길. 연인이 될 줄 알고 함께 걷는 가슴 큰 여인.
　가슴을 사고 있는 코트 속에는 많은 색다른 자존심이 들어있는 듯 푸짐하다. 잘 길들여진 얼굴인데 재갈이 물려있다. 심한 자존심이 새어나오지 않게 하려 함일까. 이토록 불안하게 함께 걸어도 슬퍼지지는 않았다. 가끔 아는 사람 만나면 데스마스크를 쓰고 지나갔다.

　하늘이 수많은 별들을 혼자 보려고 어두움 속 깊숙이 숨겨 두는 이유를 알았다. 태초 이전에 있을 허공 속에서 떨어진 한 방울의 그리움이 바로 그대. 내 육신과 영혼에서만 피어나게 하고 싶은 욕망의 달빛으로 밤길을 걷는다. 그댄 달빛 맞으려 황홀한 가슴을 연다.

　행복하게 향취를 맡으며 밤길을 걸었지만 나 혼자 걷는 것을 깨달았을 때 꽃은 저만치 뒤에 서 있었다. 서 있기만 했다. 마음으로는 따라와야 하는 것을 알면서도 모질게 모질게 거부해야만 기다리지 않겠지 생각하면서 속으로는 울면서 하얀 증오심과 자존심을 들추어 보인다. 나의 생에 단 한 번밖에 없는 아름다운 행운을 세월의 마지막 책갈피를 넘길 때까지 넘치지 않게 슬프도록 고이 간직하련다.

(2013년 4월 21일)

# Evening Primrose

There is a path where flowers burn their flames of desire in the dark.
Women with large breasts that walk thinking they are now lovers.
The coat that covers her breasts looks full with a number of different prides.
The face has good contours, but bites down on a gag.
Maybe it's so that her big ego will not be exposed.
Even as they walk together so uneasily, it is not sad.
When a person she knows passes by, it wears a death mask and passes by.

I learned the reason why the heavens hide the numerous stars is to see it for itself. You are the drop of longing that was dropped in the space even before the beginning. I walk the streets in the night with the moonlight of desire, so that it may blossom only in my body and my soul. You open your mesmerizing breast to greet the moonlight.

I walk the night streets filled with happiness and smelling your scent, but when I realize that I walk alone, the flower still stands far back. It only stands. Though it knows at heart that it must follow, it thinks that it must refuse so that it will not wait, but inside it cries and reveals white hatred and pride. I want to sadly keep the beautiful fortune that will come only once in my life, until the last page in time.

(April 21, 2013)

# 나이테

잘려진 허리에서
수백 년 침략에 맞서 넓혀간 영토의 성벽이 동심원을 그린다.
헤아릴 수 없이 많은 잎을 가진 나무들이
영욕의 세월을 나누어 가며 욕망의 선을 긋는다.
용감한 부하를 거느린 광개토대왕,
살수대첩의 을지문덕과 같은
역사의 많은 잎들이 떨어지며 새겨 놓은 무늬는
세월이 흐를수록 아름답다.
삶의 목표를 삼든지, 큐비트 화살의 과녁이 되든지
아직도 애족愛族의 눈물을 퍼내는 물레방아는 끊임없이 도는데
그 속에는
세월이 있고,
그리움이 산다.

(2013년 4월 24일)

# Tree Rings

From a severed waist,
the castle walls of territory that defeated hundreds of years of invasion draw concentric circles.
The trees with countless leaves
draw lines of desire as they share times of glory and shame.
Like King Gwanggaeto who ruled over courageous vassals,
and Uljimundeok of the Battle of Salsu,
the patterns drawn, as numerous leaves that fell in history
become more beautiful as time passes.
Whether it becomes a goal of life or a target for Cupid's arrow,
the watermill that draws the tears of love for one's nation continue to row,
and in it
is the time that passed,
and in it lives longing.

(April 24, 2013)

# 어느 곰팡이의 서식棲息

　어느 문화교실에서
온 힘을 다해 두 해 동안 텃밭을 일구었다.
만일 기계도 쓰다가 고장 나면 수리를 하는데
내가 눈이 아파 두 주를 병원에서 쉬고 왔다.
현실은 참으로 냉혹했다.
개척자는 슬펐다.

　광활한 미생물계微生物界에서
안착 못해 떠돌던 늙은 곰팡이 하나
공생할 기주寄主에 붙어 텃밭에 내렸다.
　다시 황원荒原으로 만들어 버린 곰팡이는 자라는 식물 더러
'길이 아닌 데는 가지도 말라'고 입으로 거품을 내놓으며
텃밭을 황폐하게 만들었다.
　요즈음은 불도저로 길이 아닌 곳도 길을 내는 세상인
데⋯⋯.

　언젠가 정상적인 천이遷移가 올 것인지
　곰팡이의 노욕老慾만 서식한다.

# Habitat of a Mold

At a culture class
I cultivated a garden for two years with all my might.
When a machine I used broke, I fixed it,
but my eyes hurt, so I spent two weeks in the hospital.
Reality was cold.
The pioneer was sad.

An old mold that could not find refuge
in a vast world of microorganisms
found a host and made my garden its home.
The mold that returned to the wastelands said to the plants,
"Don't go where there is no path," with bubbles in its mouth, and then ruined the garden.
This is despite the fact that paths can be made with bulldozers where there are none...

Perhaps normal succession will come some day,
but for now it is a habitat only for the old greed of a mold.

# 양파

세속의 그늘에서 옷을 벗긴다
더러운 손으로
위정자爲政者일까, 탕아蕩兒일까?

세균이 득실거리는 손톱을 깎지 않는 체
속살을 더듬으며
거짓이 가득한 욕망으로 옷을 벗긴다

돈이나 권력의 그늘에서 자란
탐욕의 세균으로 오염된
가증스런 손으로 옷을 벗긴다

분명, 양파는 아프다
소리칠 수 없는 수치심에 떨며
그늘에서 묻혀 온 세균을 받아들인다

한 겹 한 겹 썩어가는 양파
벗을 옷조차 소진되고
심연에 간직한 삶의 알맹이조차 없다

# Onion

He takes off its clothes
With dirty hands
Is he a politician or a debaucher?

Without cutting the nails, swarming with bacteria
Feeling the skin
He takes off its clothes with a desire full of lies

Grown up in the shadow of money or power
Contaminated with the bacteria of greed
With the contemptible hand, he takes off its clothes

Certainly, the onion is in pain
Trembling with the shame of being unable to shout
It accepts the bacteria smeared in the shadow

The onion that is rotting layer by layer
Even the clothes to take off have been exhausted
And there is no kernel of life kept in the abyss

이제, 벗기는 자가 벗어야 할 때
옷은 있으되 벗을 수 없고
육신은 있으되 입을 옷이 없다

매운 눈물만 흘릴 뿐이다

(2010년 10월 22일)

Now, it's time for the one who takes off to take off his clothes
Though he has clothes, he cannot take them off
Though there is a body, there are no clothes to wear

He just sheds spicy tears

                                                (October 22, 2010)

# 갈대 소리

비비어만 아는가
그대 사랑을

살갗이 맞닿아서 내는 소리는
비통하게 서거기는 신음소리뿐

왼 종일 피부가 맞닿아도 느끼는 건
식어버린 가슴

공해로 바랜 흰머리로 통곡하는
낙동강 갈대 소리에 익어가는 석양만 슬프다

# Sound of reeds

Can I know only by rubbing?
Your love

The sound made by skins in contact with each other is
Only groans that crunch sadly

Even when the skins are in contact with each other all day, what I feel is
The heart that has cooled down

Crying bitterly with white hair faded by pollution
At the sound of reeds along the Nakdong River, only the ripening setting sun is sad

# 은행잎

싸늘한 외면에
요절한 시인

읊다가 못 읊어
던져버린 원고原稿

흙탕물에 젖고 밟혀
내 속의 얼룩 같은 잎새

못다 한 사랑이
노랗게 아프다

(2010년 11월 27일)

# Ginkgo Leaves

Due to cold turning away
The poet died young

Tried to read but unable to read
The manuscript was thrown away

Soaked with muddy water and stepped upon
Leaves that are like the stains in me

The uncompleted love is
Painful and yellowish

(November 27, 2010)

# 배추의 귀

배추는 귀가 있다
연둣빛 자태를 뽐내며 서늘한 가을에 서서
주인의 발자국 소릴 듣고 자란다

머언 옛날
어미도 아비도 그러했듯이
죽을 수도 없는 휴면기간을 넘겨야 싹을 틔우는 것을
기억하고 있는가

애써 주인이 갈고 부수어 놓은
부드러운 땅 기운을 받고
뿌리를 내려야 했던 고뇌들
무엇으로 보답해야 할지 고민하며 살아온 것을
기억하고 있는가

삶 속에 몰아닥칠 엘니뇨나 라니냐가 얼마나 괴롭힐지
삶이 사치가 아닌지 번민하여 보았는가
너의 귀를 쫑긋 세워라
주인이 오는 발자국 소리를 들을 수 있게
귀가 있는 배추만 살아남기에

# Ears of Chinese cabbage

Chinese cabbage has ears
Boasting about their yellowish green figures and standing in the cool autumn
They grow hearing the steps of the owner

A long time ago
As did mother and father
Do you remember
That you can bud only after passing a period of dormancy when you cannot even die

The agonies about the fact that you had to
receive the soft energy of the earth
Elaborately plowed and broken into pieces by the owner to the your roots
Do you remember
That you have lived deeply thinking about how you can pay for it

How much will the El Nino or La Nina that would come into

건강하게 자라서
육신을 받쳐 영혼을 깨끗하게 할 수 있다면
오히려 영광이련만
세월은 그냥 두지 않는 것을…….

네 앞에 주인의 낫과 괭이가 보이는구나.


(2011년 1월 5일 수요일 정오)

your life torment you

Whether your life is luxury or not, did you undergo a mental conflict

Prick up your ears

So that you can hear the steps of your owner coming

Since only those Chinese cabbages that have ears survive

If you can grow healthily

To sacrifice your body in order to clean up your soul

It will be an honor

But time does not leave you as you are······.

In front of you are seen your owner's sickle and pick.

(At noon, January 5, 2011, Wednesday)

# 동구 밖 정자나무

홀로 피기조차 힘겨운
소녀 시절
의지할 곳 없어 헤매며
찾아온 정자나무

하늘은 뿌옇게 안개에 가렸고
삶의 애절함도 낯선 이야기
진종일 울먹이다
부어오른 눈

기구한 운명이 기다리는 줄
누가 알았으랴
동구 밖 정자나무 아래에
신음하는 철부지 아이

아버지 보고파서 찾아간 날은
알지 못할 슬픔만 가득 안고서
큰 나무 아래로 발길을 옮겨
외로이 지새던 수많은 밤

# A Shade Tree at the Outskirts of the Village

Hard even to bloom alone
In her childhood
While wandering since there was no place to rely on
She came to a shade tree

The sky was covered by foggy mist
At a story in which the sorrow of life is unfamiliar
After being about to cry all day
The eyes swelled up

That a strange fate was waiting
Who did know
Under the shade tree at the outskirts of the village
An immature child is moaning

On days when the child visited her father, who she wanted to see
Embracing only unknown sorrow fully in her arms
She went below the large tree
To stay up alone all through the numerous nights

마음을 가다듬고 돌아와 본들
아무도 반겨줄 이 없는
공허한 방에
희미한 등불만 새어 나온다

수십 년 하루처럼 지나간 후
고향이 그리워 돌아 와보니
동구 밖 나무는 그대로인데
모두가 변해버린 낯선 사람뿐

지금은 두 아이 엄마가 되어도
혼자라는 외로운 생각만 들어
고단한 삶의 길 왜 이리 긴지
잠든 남편 물끄러미 바라만 본다

차라리 무인도에 갇혀 살아도
외로움과 슬픔을 벗어버리고
진종일 새들과 노래 부르며
예쁜 꽃잎 듬뿍 따서
그녀의 마음에 뿌려주고 싶다.

(2010년 1월 18일, 어느 여인의 독백)

From the vacant room
Where there is no one to greet her
Even when she come back after calming herself down
Only vague lamplight shines through the chinks of the door

When several decades had passed by in a flash
She missed her hometown and came back
Though the tree at the outskirts of the village was as it had been
All the people were unfamiliar

Now, although she has become a mother of two children
She just feels lonely thinking that she is alone and
Not knowing why the tiresome journey of life is so long
She just looks at her sleeping husband vacantly

Even if I have to live on an uninhabited island
After taking off loneliness and sorrow
Singing with birds all day
After picking an armful of beautiful floral leaves
I would like to scatter on her mind.

(January 18, 2010, a monologue of a woman)

# 해바라기

해바라기는 씨앗을 위해
굴욕의 몸짓으로
태양을 향한다

신의 영역조차 침식하는
교활한 인간은
쭉정이만 품은 해바라기이런가

높은 곳만 쳐다보며
굽실대던 육신
부끄러운 하늘만 높다

가식은 태양의 빛을 잃게 하고
높이 쌓은 과학은
신神이 필요 없다지만

메마른 억새풀 사이를 지나는
세월조차 멈추지 못하는
아둔한 인간의 허망함이 슬프다

# Sunflower

To grow seeds, sunflowers
Face the sun
With humiliating gestures

Eroding even the domain of God
Are cunning humans
Sunflowers that have only empty grains

Only looking up at high places
The body that was crawling
Only the shameful sky is high

Though they say false pretenses make the sun lose its light
And highly accumulated science
Does not need God

The vanity of stupid humans
Who cannot even stop time
That passes through dried flame grass, is sad

향할 곳 없는 어둠만이
희망의 실오라기를 별에서 뽑으려
밤의 물레를 잣고 있다

(2011년 1월 18일)

Only the darkness that has nowhere to go
Is turning a spinning wheel of night
In order to spin the thread of hope from stars


                                            (January 18, 2011)

# 꽃가루의 꿈

나의 꽃가루를
바람으로 보낼까
벌·나비에 부칠까

구름에 실려 가도
빗물에 흘러가도
그대를 잊을 수 없어

분홍 꽃 암술에 내려
긴 관으로 그대의 씨방에서
나의 유전자를 발현하고 싶다

식어가는 지표에
새싹으로 다시 움터
눈물로 이루어진
그대의 심연에 꽃으로 피련다.

(2011년 4월 17일)

# Dream of Pollen

Should I send my pollen
By wind?
Or by bee or butterfly?

I can't forget you
Even carried by a cloud
Or rain

Landing on the pistil of a pink flower
My genes pass to your ovary
Through a long tube

By sprouting
On a cooled indicator
I would like to blossom in your abyss
Which is composed of tears

(April 17, 2011)

# 꽃가루 알레르기


정욕에 불태운 오월
수컷들의 정자들
온 천지에 난자를 찾아 유영遊泳타가
제구실도 못해 비에 씻겨
시멘트 바닥에 어지럽게 노랗다

황홀하고 달콤한 탐욕의 유혹은
향내를 지닌 체
코와 눈을 침입한
이 못난 정자들
분명히 자위 행동의 결과다

일생을
남에게 고통을 주어
즐거워하는 무리들
페르소나의 탈을 쓴 이리다.

# Pollen Allergy

In May, which burned with lust
The sperm
Sought eggs from all over
But failed and was washed out by the rain
Leaving a yellow mass on the cement floor

The allure of blissful and sweet lust
Is the ultimate result of masturbation
Of this useless sperm
That invades noses and eyes
With a foul scent

A group that finds happiness
By giving pain to others
Throughout their lives
Are wolves in disguise

진정한 사랑으로 맺어진 생명이
태어나려
씨방이 찢어지는 고통을 햇볕에 달구어
무지개 닮은 세월 위에
촘촘히 유월의 잎새를 연다.

(2011년 5월 7일)

A life born of true love
Opens the fine leaves of June
Into a time resembling a rainbow
By burning the pain of a torn ovary, under the sunlight

(May 7, 2011)

# 숟가락으로 퍼먹는 들판


많은 물들이 가득 담겨 있는 벌판을 지난다.

좁은 의자에 발 뻗을 틈 없는 15인승 자동차
길을 잃고 헤매다 제 길을 찾아가는 번복된 운전
네모진 파아란 들판은 자꾸 지나가나
운전대에 매달린 긴장감은 사라지고
다정함이 깔깔대는 웃음과 함께 풍요로 변해
가슴으로 흘러든다.

삶의 벽이 시간 위에서 달리다 허물어지고
이제, 가는 길조차 여유로운 시인詩人이 되어
가는 목적지가 어디든 상관이 없다
그 위를 갈 수 있게 뻗쳐 있으면 된다.

일찍 핀 동백이 말을 한다.
'너희들 아무리 풍요롭게 이 들판을 차지해도
숟가락 하나로 들판을 먹어버릴 것을'
비명같이 들리는 외마디 소리
어느 노 시인의 독백獨白이다.
부함도 가난도 외길인 것을

# Scooping a Field with a Spoon

Passing through water-laden fields

A car with 15 small seats, and no places to stretch the feet
Is lost and searches for the path
After passing several square green fields
The nervousness from driving is gone
And friendliness changes to giggling abundance
Flowing into the heart

The wall of life falls down with time
And becomes like a relaxed poet
Heedless of the destination
As long as it is outstretched to go over

A camellia flower that bloomed to early says
'Although you occupy this field abundantly
You must eat it with a spoon'
It is a scream-like exclamation;
a monologue of an old poet.

흔적조차 없어질 삶의 시詩이련가
한 숟가락에 올려진 작은 인생이여!


(2011년 6월 11일)

Both richness and poverty are a single path
A poem of life that will disappear without trace
What a little life placed on a spoon!

(June 11, 2011)

# 뻐꾸기

뻐꾸기가 남의 둥지에 알을 낳았다
거침없는 성性의 난무亂舞
함께 못사는 예고된 불행이다.
품고, 먹이는 어미 박새
제 자식인 줄 알고 얼마나 기뻤을까
강한 새끼만 먹여 주는 습성뿐인데
자신의 혈육이 아래로 쫓겨나는 필연적 운명에
입 벌리고 있는 죽음의 깊은 수렁
땅은 말이 없다

끈끈한 인연도, 사랑도 아랑곳없는
둥지에는 혈연이
치열한 혼란으로 몸살을 앓고 있다.

뻐꾸기 새끼는
남의 열정으로 자라난 것도 모르는 채
홀가분한 마음으로 날아간다.
아무도 입을 열지 않는다.

(2013년 4월 26일)

# Cuckoo

A cuckoo laid eggs in another's nest.
A wild dance of relentless sex.
It was an expected misfortune of not being able to live together.
The mother's great tit that cared for it and fed it,
how happy it must have been believing it to be its child.
Their nature is to feed only their strong children.
In their nature to chase away their own blood,
to the deep pits of death that opens its mouth.
The land says nothing.

In the loveless and relationship-less
nest, are blood ties
that ache in fierce confusion.

The baby cuckoo
growing without knowing the passion of a stranger,
leaves the nest with an easy mind.
Nobody says anything.

(April 26, 2013)

# 매미

칠흑 같은 본능 속에 갇힌 긴 세월
벗어버린 가증한 옷
욕망으로 터져버린 등背에 한 겹의 생애가 슬프다

겹눈이 아무리 튀어나와도
정욕이 육신만 껴안고 살아야 하기에
애닯게 울고 있다.

어쩌면 홑눈으로
빈혈을 앓고 있는 진실 된 영혼을 볼 수 있으련만
습관화되어버린 무관심無關心

목구멍으로 울 자격조차 없어
허구虛構로 채워버린 복부腹部로
수컷만 울어야 한다.

이토록 한여름 밤이 가까이 오는데
고난苦難의 못 자국 닮은 세 개의 홑눈을 숨긴 채
갈망渴望의 늪에서 수컷은 울고 있다.

(2012년 4월 11일)

# Cicada

A long time bonded by a dark instinct.
The abominable clothes that were taken off.
The layer of life on a back that exploded with desire is pitiful.

No matter how much its compound eyes bulge,
because its lust must live embracing only its body,
it cries sadly.

Maybe with a simple eye,
if it could see the true soul suffering from anemia,
but indifference has become habit.

Not having what it takes to cry with its throat,
using its abdomen filled with nothingness,
the male has to cry.

A mid-summer night comes so close,
hiding its three simple eyes that resemble traces of a pond of hardship,
the male cries in a swamp of eager desires.

(April 11, 2012)

# 진딧물

기나긴 질고疾苦의 시간 지나
새 하늘 맞는 어린 새순의 혈관에
피를 빤다

눈물도 동정도 없다
오직 눈앞에 보이는 이익을 위해
패거리를 만든다.

얼마나 바빴기에 따뜻한 계절엔
섹스도 필요 없이 암컷은 암컷만 낳는다.
수컷이 필요 없는 처녀생식處女生殖

도덕도, 인격도 필요 없다
항문에서 내어 놓는 달콤한 맛에
배만 채울 숱한 개미만 모여든다.

신神이 버린 오물汚物인가
악마惡魔의 덫인가
중독中毒된 인간의 해충들.

(2012년 4월 12일)

# Aphid

After the passing of a long sickness,
it sucks the blood
from the veins of a young shoot that greets the new sky.

It sheds no tears and has no sympathy.
Only for the spoils in front of its eyes,
it gangs up.

It is so busy that even in the warm seasons,
without the need of sex, females give birth only to females.
A parthenogenesis that needs men not.

It has no ethics and no character.
Its sweet taste from its anus
gathers only ants that wish to fill their stomachs.

Is it waste thrown away even from god,
or is it a trap of the devil,
these pests of poisoned humans.

(April 12, 2012)

# 누에

점點 같은 생명으로 세상에 왔건만
낳아준 어머니를 볼 수가 없어
외로이 눈물로 지새우는 밤

자꾸만 보고 싶은
내 어머니
잊으려 잊으려 잠을 청請한다

잠에서 일어나
근심과 시련의 옷 벗어 버려도
그리움만 가슴에 짙게 물든다.

우리의 나래에 깃털 만들려
1,500미터의 하얀 연緣줄
오늘도 쉬지 않고 뽑고 뽑지만

그리움의 고치에 갇혀버린 나
꿈에라도 엄마 손을 잡고 있으면
나도 어머니 닮아 하늘을 난다

(2012년 4월 14일)

# Silkworm

It came to the world as a speck-like life form.
But because it cannot see its mother
it spends its nights with lonely tears.

It always longs
for its mother,
but it seeks sleep to forget, to forget.

As it arises from sleep
and even after taking off its clothes of worry and hardship,
only longing paints its heart.

To make the feathers to our wings,
the white strings spanning 1,500 meters,
it spins without rest even today.

It is tied down in a cocoon of longing,
if it can hold its mother's hand, even if it is but a dream,
it also flies away like its mother.

(April 14, 2012)

# 달팽이

길을 내기가 너무 더딥니다.
빨리 달려가고 싶어도
내 안에는 두 가지 마음이 있기 때문입니다.

한 길을 못 가고 뒤뚱이는 육신에
한몸에 자웅雌雄 생식기를 가져야 하는
자연의 섭리가 내리는 형벌刑罰

끈적거리는 고통의 길을
그 무거운 집조차 짊어지고 끙끙대며
사랑하는 자를 찾아 헤맵니다.

오직,
선과 악이 공존하는 마음이 괴로워
질고의 거품이 이는 습지에서 살아야 하는 운명

모든 아픔 훌훌 벗어던지고
외로워도
저 찬란한 햇볕 속을 거닐고 싶습니다.

(2012년 4월 23일)

# Snail

It takes too long to make a path.
Though my desire is to run fast,
I cannot because of the two desires in me.

In an awkward body that cannot go one path
and being a hermaphrodite,
this is the punishment given by Mother Nature.

In the sticky path of pain,
having to huff and puff wearing a heavy home,
I am in search of the person I love.

Only,
my heart in which good and evil coexist is painful,
and I am destined to live in a swamp of bubbles of despair.

I wish to cast away all my pains,
and even if it means being lonely,
I wish to walk amidst the radiant sunlight.

(April 23, 2012)

# 공벌레

나보다 더 큰 힘 앞에
죽은 척
위선偽善의 의태擬態로
위기를 모면謀免하는 공벌레 된다.

실패와 절망이 다가오면
수많은 다리로 일어설 수 있는데도
나는 공벌레가 된다

세월의 파도를 타고 가는 인생길
즐거운 서핑으로 가야 하는데
때때로 다리를 몸뚱이에 넣고 공이 된다.

근본은 동물인데
곤충의 이름을 빌어 벌레처럼 살면서
어이, 장애물을 헤쳐 가며 떳떳이 걸을까

(2012년 4월 23일)

# Pill Bug

In front of a force stronger than mine,
I play dead.
Under the guise of hypocrisy,
I become a pill bug that overcome crises.

When there is failure and despair,
though I have many legs to stand back up on,
I become a pill bug.

The walk of life that surfs on the waves of times,
should be a fun surf,
but sometimes I put my legs under my body and become a ball.

Though I am by nature an animal,
I borrow the name of an insect and live like a bug.
Hey, why not overcome obstacles and live proud?

(April 23, 2012)

## 무당벌레



새순의 피를 빨아먹는 진딧물을 배웠음인가
어린 가슴에 매달려 흡혈하는 군상들
메말라가는 줄기마다 한恨이 서린다

무당벌레야!
몹쓸 진딧물 같은 치한癡漢을 찾으려
붉은 갑옷에 검은 수류탄을 군데군데 짊어지고
뒷날개에 프로펠러를 달고 빨리 날아라.

순진한 소녀를 위안부로 만들고
죽도란 이름 붙여
짓밟고, 점령하려는 야욕의 독초들

너의 경계색을 보고
저어 파렴치한 족속들이 오금을 못 필 때
멸종시켜 버려라

정녕,
너는 그들의 천적으로 군림하리니
하나라도 남김없이 박멸하여 버려라

# Ladybug

Perhaps because it learned from aphids that suck the blood of shoots,
   this group that clings to young breasts and sucks its blood,
   resentment grows with each dying stem.

Ladybug!
To find the perverts like the evil aphid,
wear your black grenades on your red armor,
place a propeller on your back wings, and fly quick.

It makes innocent girls into sex slaves,
and gives them the name, "Jukdo",
to stomp and conquer them, these poisonous plants of desire.

When they see your warning colors,
and when those shameless gangs tremble in fear,
exterminate them.

Truly,
you rule over them as their natural enemy,
so exterminate each and every one of them.

# 칠성무당벌레

달을 반으로 잘라
풀 내음 스며오는 이슬에 놓고
갈증으로 검게 타들어 가는 그리움 일곱 번 찍어
알록달록한 선홍빛 외투를 입혀 주었지

그 외투 속에 신성하고 따뜻한
나의 심장을 숨겨 두었지

그녀는 알지 못하고 밖이 추울수록
자꾸만 지프를
목덜미에서 발끝까지 채우기만 했지

어느덧 나의 심장에서 혈관이 이어지고
그녀의 온몸에 나의 온기가 퍼져 나갔지
결국 그녀는 내가 되는 줄도 모르고…….

(2012년 4월 24일)

# Seven-spotted Ladybug

The moon was cut in half
and placed on dew with the fragrance of grass,
and seven dots of longing that burned black with thirst was marked,
and then was given a spotted scarlet coat.

Inside the coat was hidden
my sacred and warm heart.

She did not know
and when it became colder,
she only zipped up from head to toe.

Soon enough my heart was connected to veins,
and in her body my warmth spread,
and knew she not, that she became me……．

(April 24, 2012)

# 좀벌레

시험 칠 때면 며칠 동안 밤새워
공부해온 남의 정답을 슬쩍 훔쳐보고
자기의 답안지를 메우며 만족하는 군상群像들

요즈음은 농땡이 치는 사람이
사회에 나가면 더 잘되는 세상
공부는커녕,
데모만 열심이면 어디든지 들어간다.
좀벌레다.

지식의 천이든
데모의 천이든
입고 있는 옷이 무엇이든 간에 좀이 끓는다.

수놈의 좀벌레
교미 없이 구애求愛만 하고
정충 한 덩어리 방출하고 나면
암컷이 주워 자신의 질膣 속에 넣어버린다.
좀벌레도 시험 치나 보다

# Silverfish

While I stay up nights to study for tests
they look off my answers
and fill in their answers finding satisfaction, these gangs do.

Those who are lazy and do nothing
do better in society these days.
Rather than studying,
they do better by going on demonstrations.
They are silverfish.

Whether it is fabric of knowledge
or fabric of demonstrations,
whatever they wear, it boils me over.

The male silverfish,
it has courtship without mating,
and when it emits a lump of spermatozoon,
the female puts it in its vagina.
Maybe the silverfish is also taking a test.

며칠 후 부화한 새끼들
은빛의 옷들을 몇 벌씩 갈아입고
성충成蟲의 모습을 갖추어가며
천을 뜯어먹는 훌륭한(?) 지도자 된다.

(2012년 4월 25일)

Their babies that hatch in a couple days
changes silver clothes several times
as they become imago
and become excellent(?) leaders that eat fabric.

(April 25, 2012)

# 나방이

조용히 방에 앉아 마음 다스리는 책을 읽는데
나방 한 마리가 주위를 맴돈다. 날개를 퍼덕인다.
마음을 비우려 애쓰는 순간
나도 모르게 그 책으로 나방이를 쳤다. 버둥대다 죽었다.
잠시라도 선善 해보려 노력 중인데
순간적, 야성野性으로 전환됐다.
마음의 창을 열어줄 책을 도구로 사용한
파렴치한 행동에
책보기 민망했다.

처절하게 죽어가는 나방이 한 마리가
나를 가르쳤다. '넌, 아직 이 책을 볼 자격이 없다' 고.

(2013년 4월 28일)

# Moth

I read a book that relaxes my mind in a quiet room,
but a moth flies around me. It flutters its wings.
While trying to empty my mind,
without knowing, I hit the moth with the book. It wriggles and soon dies.
I was trying to be good for even just a moment,
but in an instant I became wild.
The book that should open the windows of my heart was used as a tool
in my shameless act,
and I felt ashamed to read the book.

The moth that was dying
taught me, 'You are not yet worthy of reading this book'.

(April 28, 2013)

# 맹꽁이 사랑


맹꽁이가 논에서 사랑을 한다

두 눈을 크게 뜨고
울음주머니 커다랗게 부풀어
수컷이 '내 님은 어디에 있나 응~아'
암컷은 '여기 있다 응~아'
긴긴 여름을 논에서 숨바꼭질한다.

맹꽁이 울음이
자라나는 벼이삭에
풍년을 심으면
물 대던 농부의 두 손이 바빠진다

한여름 밤이면 들려오는 맹꽁이 소리
무겁다 응~아
내려라 응~아
긴긴 밤의 사랑은 점점 익어만 간다.

# Narrow-Mouthed Toad's Love

Narrow-mouthed toads make love in a field

With eyes wide open
With bloated vocal sacks
"Where are you, honey, Eng~Ah" says male
"Here I am, Eng~Ah" says female
They spend the summer playing hide and seek in the field

When planting the harvest
On ears of rice
Where the narrow-mouthed toad's crying grows
Watering farmers hands become busy

Narrow-mouthed toad's crying sound on a summer night
Heavy Eng-Ah
Get down Eng-Ah
Their love of long nights becomes ripe

논을 떠난 맹꽁이
생태공원 미명 아래 바꿔버린 자유로
인디언보호구역
생각이 난다

괴롭다 응~아
어떻게 살고 응~아
들려오는 한탄 소리
여름을 장식한다.

(2011년 7월 16일)

Narrow-mouthed toads left the field
From the freedom given under the guise of ecological park
Like the Indian Reservations

It's painful Eng-Ah
How should we live Eng-Ah
Their lamenting sound
Decorates the summer

(July 16, 2011)

# 공생共生

더러운 바람둥이의 유전자 받기 싫어
여름이 되면
진딧물은 처녀로 새끼를 낳는다.

가눌 길 없는 무거운 몸
부드러운 잎이나 줄기에 옮겨주고
개미는 진딧물의 달콤한 당분을 취한다.

개미는 결코 더러운 유전자는
취하지 않는다.

미물微物조차 상리공생相利共生하는데
상생相生 하나 못하는
잡식성雜食性의 사람이 부끄럽다.

(2011년 8월 8일)

# Symbiosis

Hate to receive casanova's dirty genes
When the summer comes
The virginal Aphid brings forth its young

Too heavy to hold itself
Provided with soft leaves or stems
Ants take the sweet sugar of the aphid

Ants never take
Dirty genes

Even little parts of symbiosis
Shame that the polyphagial human
Can not be symbiotic

(August 8, 2011)

### 제2장

# 자연의 숨소리

### Chapter 2

# Breath of Nature

# 가야산 기슭에서


늦가을
안개 피어오르는 가야산 기슭에서
그대 만나지 않았더라면
나는 아직도 다른 세상을 알지 못하였을 것입니다.

모든 생명을 품고 있는 산
탁한 것을 정화시키는 그곳에서
한 번이라도 호흡하지 않았더라면
나는 질식되어 삶의 무호흡증에서 헤어나지 못하였을 것입니다.

종종 헛디딘 발이 삐어져 아파도
그곳에 오르지 않았으면
시련과 고통이 얼마나 성숙하게 만드는지를 모르는 채
온실 속에 갇혀있는 나무로 자랐을 것입니다.

밖에 나와 시들어 버리거나
열매를 맺는다 한들
도깨비바늘처럼 지나가는 사람들의 옷에 붙어
다른 곳에서 정처 없이 살려고만 애썼겠지요.

# At the Foot of Gayasan(Mt.)

Late fall,
at the foot of Gayasan where the fogs rise,
had I not met you,
I would still not know of the other world.

The mountain that embraces all life,
at this place that purifies all that is dirty,
if I had not breathed here once,
I would have been strangled and become prisoner to the apnea of life.

Even if I lose my footing and sprain my ankle,
if I had not climbed this mountain,
I would not know that trials and pains help mature,
and grow as a tree in a greenhouse.

Even if I came outside and withered
or if I gave fruits,
I would have stuck onto the clothes of people passing by like Spanish needles,
and tried to live without knowing where to go.

오늘도
안개구름 피어나는 산기슭에서
슬프도록 그리운 그대 생각에
가슴 가득 산을 안고 걸어갑니다.

(2013년 4월 27일)

Again today,
in the foot of the mountain where the fogs rise,
I think of you who I sadly long for,
and walk with the mountain in my heart.

(April 27, 2013)

# 잃어버린 시간을 찾아

유인원들이 미래시대에 와 있다.
돌도끼를 들고 덤벼들 기세氣勢에
눈빛과 자세가 당당한 나신裸身.
오히려 현란한 옷으로 욕망을 가린 현대인이 부끄럽다.
아담과 이브도 육신의 일부분을 가렸지만
인간이 신神과 교합交合할 수 있는 같은 DNA를 가졌을 때는
육신에 짊어질 수치심羞恥心의 멍에도 없었을 게다.
이제, 시간조차 벗어버린 영혼이 부럽다.
잃어버린 시대의 한 토막을 그리워하며 낙원 밖 외지에서
로켓으로 쏘아 올리는 열망熱望이란 위성들
언어를 흩어버린 바벨탑 같다.
내가 만든 삶 속에 벗고 다닐 정원이라도 있었으면
위선과 오만傲慢으로 덧칠되어있지 않았을 텐데
폐광廢鑛의 땅굴 속
박물관에 벗은 군상群像에는
화려한 언어로 마음을 수繡놓거나,
가식假飾의 꽃들이 자라지 않는다.

# In Search of Lost Time

Anthropoids have come to the future.

Their vigor, as if they will attack with stone axes,

and naked bodies with confident eyes and posture.

I am ashamed of modern man who hides their desires with brilliant clothing.

Though Adam and Eve also covered part of their bodies,

when humans had the DNA to walk together with god,

they would also not have had the yoke of shame that their body had to bear.

Now, I envy the soul that has taken off the clothes of time.

From outside paradise, longing for an interval from a lost age,

satellites of desire fired off in rockets

are like the Babel Tower that dispersed different tongues.

If I had a garden where I could be naked in the life I make,

I would not be covered with hypocrisy and arrogance.

Inside the cave of an abandoned mine,

the many naked people in the museum

are not embroidered with extravagant language

and it does not give blossom to the flowers of pretense.

근육에는 자유와 평화가 꿈틀대고
원시시대에 신神과의 대화가 들리는 듯하다.
벗은 자는 진정한 낙원의 소유자다.
굴 밖에서 밀려오는 소리는 안개로 변하여 엄습해오고
불경스런 유혹으로 낙원에서 쫓겨나듯
나의 발길은 어느덧 잃어버린 시간을 지나 밖으로 나온다.
황홀한 옷들이 떼 지어 다니는 길목에
흔들리며 변해가는 시간이 나의 등을 떠민다.


(2013년 2월 1일, 울산 언양 작천정 동굴박물관에서)

My muscles squirm with freedom and peace
and I feel like I can hear the dialogue of gods in the primitive ages.
The naked person is the true steward of paradise.
The sounds from outside the cave are turned into fog as it creeps in,
and as if to be evicted from paradise through impious temptations,
my feet pass the lost time and go back outside.
In the crossroad where there are groups of extravagant clothing,
the time that shakes and changes prods me from the back.

(February 1, 2013, At the Jakcheonjeong Cave Museum in Eonyang, Ulsan)

## 교신交信


인공위성人工衛星을 쏘아 올린다고,
궤도 진입한다고
성공이 아니다
우주본부와 교신을 해야 성공이다.
신神은 지구로 인간을 보냈다
신神을 닮은 위성衛星으로…
겸손이 어느덧 교만으로 변하여
언어 속에,
표정 속에,
행동 속에 스며있다.
잃어버린 진로進路로 우글거리는 우주쓰레기로 전락되어
교신交信이 안 된다. 궤도이탈이다.
극지방의 빙하가 녹고 오존층이 난잡하게 뚫린다.
바다에서 떠오른 달은 소금물에 젖어
퉁퉁 부어오른 커다란 얼굴로 어둠에 중독된 인간을 본다.
환락가의 찬란한 불빛은 죽음으로 향하는 탄식의 행렬이
깊어지기에
 달은 창백해진다.

# Contact

Firing up a satellite,
and going into orbit,
does not mean success.
Success is when it comes into contact with the space headquarters.
God sent man to Earth
as satellites in the likeness of god...
Humility changes into arrogance,
and in language,
in expressions,
in behavior, it spreads.
It falls as lost paths and throngs of space garbage
and cannot come into contact. It is out of orbit.

The glaciers in polar extremes are melting and the ozone layer is pierced all around.

The moon that floats above the ocean is wet with salt water
and with its bloated face, it looks down upon humans addicted to darkness.

The brilliant lights of red light districts have long lines of moaning directed to death,
and so the moon becomes pale.

그래도 나는 꿈을 꾼다.
시간에서 유입된 당신의 아름다운 입술에 젖어있는 사랑의 언어가
나의 뇌리腦裏에 스며들 때
트럼펫 마우스피스에 댄 나의 입술은
광안리 해수욕장에 파도를 기쁨으로 가득 채우고
별들은 구름처럼 내려와 물결 위에 앉는다.
은파는 은하수와 교신을 하고 인간은 신神과의 교신이 시작된다.
나는 수억 광년을 넘어선 태초 이전의 당신과 교신을 한다.
우리 모두가 교신을 한다.

(2012년 2월 3일)

But dream, I still do.

When the language of love soaked in your beautiful lips from time permeates through my mind,

my lips on the trumpet mouthpiece

fill the waves of Gwangalli Beach with happiness

and the stars come down like the clouds and sit on top of the water.

The silvery moonlit waves come into contact with the galaxies and humans begin their contact with god.

I came into contact with you, a being before the beginning, billions of light years away.

We are all in contact.

(February 3, 2012)

# 달의 소묘素描

보름달이 된 지
한 주가 지났는데
벌써 왼쪽 반이 사라진 하현달이다.
젊을 때에는 생각지도 못할
나의 육신의 반을 어두움이 잠식해 간다.
시간이 갈수록
지루한 자포자기自暴自棄가
스스로 내 영혼에 무덤을 파고
고귀한 언행도 점점 그믐달이 되어 얼굴을 가린다.
영원을 다스리는 자가
그믐 같은 어둠 속에서 외로운 영혼을 위해
자그마한 촛대에 사랑을 점화하면
초승달 같은 신앙으로
어둠에서 나와
잃어버린 하현달의 왼쪽 사유思惟의 능력을 되살려
상현달로 회복게 한다.

# Drawing of the Moon

Since the full moon
it has been a week,
and it is a waning moon with half of it gone already.
What I never thought of when I was young,
half of my body is encroached by darkness.
The more time passes,
the more a boring despair
digs a grave for my soul
and noble speech and action also become a dark moon and covers my face.
He who controls his eternity,
for the lonely soul in a dark moon-like darkness,
lights love on a small candle stick.
Then a faith like a crescent moon
appears from darkness
and revives the ability of thought on the left side of the waning moon that was lost,
to restore it into a young moon.
And soon enough,

어느덧,
삶이 보름달 되어 어둠을 밀어내고
날마다 시작하는 하루가 회문回文, palindromes되어
멈추지 않는 달의 주기週期가 된다.

(2013년 2월 5일)

life becomes a full moon to push aside darkness,
and the day that begins everyday becomes palindromes
and becomes the unending cycle of the moon.

(February 5, 2013)

# 상현上弦달

한쪽이 밝으면 다른 쪽이 어둡다

거룩한 성직자의 뒤뜰에서
위선僞善의 검은 손에 성性을 유린당하는
슬픈 영혼들이 있다면
박제된 사랑에 피멍이 들어
어둠은 밝음을 잠식蠶食해 간다.
추녀 끝에 매달린 고드름이 흘리는 눈물만큼
고통이 줄어들기 위해서는
각자의 몸을 이루는 세포들과
이해와 융화融和로서 살아가야 하는 데도
좌우左右 반으로 나누어져 버린 두개골,
한편의 검은 빈 바가지 속에는
오만으로 썩어버린 오물에
절름발이 사고思考로 이루어진 구더기만 득실거린다.
머잖아 팽개쳐질 냄새 나는 바가지

# Young Moon

When one side is bright, the other is dark.

In the backyard of a holy clergy,
if there are sad souls
exploited for sex from the dark hands of hypocrisy,
bruises are inflected in stuffed love
and darkness encroaches upon brightness.
Like the tears shed by the icicles hanging from the corner of eaves,
in order to reduce pain,
the cells that make up the body
must live together with understanding and integration,
but the skull is separated into two halves,
and in one side is a dark bowl
filled with sewage, rotting with arrogance
and maggots made of crippled thoughts.
The bowl that will soon be thrown away,

파킨슨병에 걸린 손마저
펜pen의 브레이크를 못 잡고 원고지 위를 누빈다.
가라지와 곡식은 공존을 한다
뽑아야 할 가라지가 더 잘 자라기에
곡식도 뽑힐까 걱정되는 농부
추수 때만 기다리며 지켜보고 있다.
상현달의 어두운 부분은 점점 작아지고
보름달을 향해 환하게 환하게 길을 간다.

(2013년 2월 6일)

the hand inflicted with Parkinson's disease
cannot put on the brakes and the pen dances on the paper.
Foxtail and grain live together.
Because the foxtail that must be weeded grows better,
the farmer is worried that the grains will also be weeded,
so he waits until harvest.
The dark part of the young moon continues to become smaller,
and it is on its way to the brightness of the full moon.

(February 6, 2013)

# 달빛

많은 세월 지나도
향긋한 줄 장미 향내가 꿈속에 스며들 때
그대 향한 수줍음이 가슴을 저민다.

빌딩 숲 사이 흘러든 그대 하얀 옷자락
닿을 듯 말 듯 나의 손끝에
나부끼는 설레임

그댄,
하얀 버선발로 춤추는
천상의 무희舞姬

흥에 겨운 장고杖鼓 소리에
휘감아 오르는 열정은
하얗게 밀려오는 그리움의 포말泡沫

# Moonlight

Even after a long time,
when fragrant climbing roses permeate into my dreams,
my bashfulness to you hurts my heart.

Your white skirt that flows between the forest of buildings,
just at the end of my fingertips,
there is a stream of excitement.

You,
dancing in white stockings,
are a dancer of the heavens.

With the exciting sounds of the janggo drums,
the passion that rises up
is the foam of longing that crashes in as white waves.

아름다운 추억의 편린片鱗들이
별빛에 반짝이며 지새는 밤
흐르는 세월이 서러워 달은 구름 뒤에 숨는다.

어느덧 시샘하는 스산한 바람이 달빛을 몰아내고
이제, 밤의 향연饗宴이 막 끝날 즈음
꿈을 여는 창가에 내일의 해가 뜬다

(2013년 2월 7일)

Parts of beautiful memory

stay the night as the stars sparkle,

and saddened with the passing of time, the moon hides behind the clouds.

The jealous winds chase away the moonlight,

and as the feast of night comes to an end,

the sun of tomorrow rises in the window frame that opens up dreams.

(February 7, 2013)

# 메마른 계곡


싱싱한 계절에 깨끗한 물이 흐르는 깊은 산
폭포수가 흐를 때마다 희열의 신음으로 가득 찬 계곡에
찬란한 무지갯빛이 서린 안개는 세월에 쫓겨
정다운 기억들을 희미한 포말로 밀어낸다.

지금
메마른 계곡 따라 산을 오르면
바윗돌의 살갗은 검게 타고 풀숲은 통곡한다.
바람을 탄 낙엽이 스치고 지나간 상흔(傷痕)이 가물가물하다

계곡의 물은 지하수 되어 오랜 세월 땅속을 흐르면서
돌 속에 숨어있는 광물을 녹여내었지만
"나는 여행자!"
이 말 외에 무엇을 생각했을까?

많은 세월 지나도
군데군데 모여 있는 작은 웅덩이에
떠나야 할 내색도 못한 마음으로
꼬리만 자맥질하는 고추잠자리 된다.

(2013년 2월 23일)

# Dry Valley

A mountain in the deep where clean water flows in the fresh seasons,
whenever water from the falls flow, the valley is filled with moans of ecstasy.
The mist reflecting a brilliant rainbow is chased by time
and the pleasant memories are pushed away as faint bubbles.

Now,
when climbing up the mountain along the dry valley,
the surface of stones are burnt black and the grass forest cries.
There are traces of scars where leaves blown by the wind passed.

Waters of valleys become groundwater and flow underneath the earth,
and it has melted away the minerals hidden inside the stones.
But, "I am a traveler!"
Why can I not think of anything else to say except this?

Though ages have passed,
in this small puddle that gathers here and there,
unable to hint that it must leave,
it becomes a red dragonfly that dives only its tail.

(February 23, 2013)

# 눈물이 흘러내린 계곡

수많은 발자국을 남긴 계곡은 앓고 있다. 강제로 나무를 심으려는 삽질에 흙이 파헤쳐져 땅이 헐었지만 나무들에게 물을 주며 살았다. 생존의 뿌리를 내리게 하는 것이 무척 힘이 들었고, 계곡에 한 번이라도 속 시원하게 물이 가득 흐르지 못한 아픔이 허약한 희생으로 전락轉落되었다.

계곡 따라 무성한 수풀 사이에 흐르는 물이 모여 폭포수로 바위를 적실 때 수천 년 이어온 신비의 노래가 연주된다.

메말라가는 차가운 계곡물에 종종 발을 적시면 물속에 잠든 조각구름들이 놀라 산산이 흩어지고 잔잔하던 수면水面에 파문破紋이 높다. 두려운 것은, 언젠가 깊은 수렁으로 떨어져야하는 낙하落下의 법칙을 인식해야 한다.

어느덧 모진 바람에 나뭇잎은 떨어지고 영원까지 흐를 줄 알았던 폭포수는 줄어들며, 주위 환경이 공해로 채워지기 시작했다. 계곡은 면역성이 약해져 가고 나무와 수풀은 하나씩 떠나버렸다. 엉클하게 드러난 바닥에 자갈과 바위가 세찬 바람만 맞을 뿐이다. 가끔 자갈과 바위 사이에서 새어나온 눈물만 계곡 사이를 흐른다.

(2013년 2월 24일)

# Valley of Tears

The valley with countless footsteps is suffering. Shovels that try to force trees break up the earth and the ground is demolished, but the trees are kept alive by giving water. It was very difficult to plant roots of life, and the pain of not being able to have fresh water flowing in full, has brought it down to a frail sacrifice.

When the water that flows between the vast forests along the valley, gathers into a waterfall to soak the stones, the mystic song that has continued for a millennia plays.

When feet are soaked in the cold valley waters that are drying, the clouds sleeping in the water are surprised and scurry away, and the waves are high in the once-gentle surface. What is scary is that we must recognize the law of falling, so that it must one day fall into the deep depths.

As the winds grow fierce, the leaves fall and the waterfall that was expected to flow to eternity dwindles, and the surrounding environment begins to fill with emptiness. The immunity of the valley weakens and trees and forests leave one by one. Only the gravel and stones on the ragged floor are hit by the strong winds. Only the tears that are shed between the gravel and stones flow between the valleys.

(February 24, 2013)

# 잊지 못해

 불은 산을 먹고, 연기는 하늘을 먹는데 바람조차 온몸을 더듬다 머리채를 휘어잡고 이산 저산 휘젓고 다닌다. 멈추지 못한 질투와 분노에 핏발이 선 눈은 서슬이 붉다 못해 퍼렇다. 그리움일랑 싹조차 자라지 못하게 태워버려도 땅은 추억을 더듬어 그리움을 토하게 한다.
 다 타버린 재災 속에는 아직 온기가 남아있어 그 속에는 아직 나의 심장이 그대로 뛰고 있었다. 사랑은 남자를 아름답게 하지만 여자를 추醜하게 만든다. 비수匕首를 든 여자는 무서웠다.

 모든 불이 꺼졌지만 나무의 뿌리들은 죽지를 못한 채 연옥의 세계에서 고통을 받고 있다.
 끝없이 몰려오는 외로움은 노을에 타고 있는 고독의 몸부림이다.

 밤하늘을 바라보며
 나는 하얗게 빛나는 별이 되어 잊으려 잊으려 깜빡일 뿐이다.

(2013년 3월 10일)

# Unforgettable

Fire consumes mountains and smoke consumes the skies, and even the winds grope the entire body and grab hold of hair and flails along different mountains. Blood-shot eyes in ceaseless jealousy and rage have wrath that goes beyond red, and are blue. Though longing can be burned to ashes so that not even sprouts can grow, but the earth touches on memory and makes one vomit their longing.

There is still warmth in ashes and my heart still beats in it. Love makes man beautiful, but women ugly. The woman holding a dagger was frightening.

Though the fires died, the roots of trees could not die and suffer in the world of purgatory.

It is a struggle of solitude in which ceaseless loneliness burns in the sunset.

As I look into the night sky,
I become a shining white star to forget, to forget.

(March 10, 2013)

# 돈

앞집 여자는 다산多産을 했다. 아이들이 떠드는 소리에 너무 시끄럽다. 조용히 해달라고 핀잔을 줘도 자식자랑에 입이 마르다. 공기와 같아서 없으면 질식하고 많으면 좋아한다. 그래서 돼지꿈을 꾸면 돈이 많이 생기는 모양이다. 그런데 왜 이리 지저분하다는 생각이 머릿속을 혼란케 하는 것은 무엇일까?

돌아가는 윤전기는 바쁘게 해산解産하는 여자다. 똑같은 쌍둥이가 태어난다. 어둠 속에서 오만傲慢한 독선獨善으로 성장하여 무엇이나 할 수 있는 힘이 되지만 제각기 밖에 나가 결혼하는가 하면, 죽기도 하고, 노숙자가 되기도 한다. 한평생 살아봤자 허망한 꿈이다.

신神은 인간을 자기 모양으로 만들어서 생명을 불어넣었다. 인간이 다산多産하여 내어 놓은 피조물들은 생명이 없어 마음 속 깊이 숨겨져 있는 아픈 과거 하나라도 제대로 삭여내지 못하는데 사람은 어이 여기에만 매달리는지 세상이 노래지고 하늘도 노랗다.

(2013년 3월 10일)

# Money

The woman across the street has many children. The children's chattering was too loud. Even if I complain asking her to make them quiet, her mouth dries because of her endless boasting of her children. They are like oxygen, so she suffocates without them and is happy when there is an abundance of them. Maybe that's why when one dreams of pigs, money rolls in. Then why do such dirty thoughts wreak havoc in my mind?

The spinning rotary press is a woman that busily delivers babies. Twins were born. In darkness they grow with an arrogant self-righteousness and have the power to do anything. But when they go on their separate ways and become married, they die or become homeless. Their entire lives are but futile dreams.

God gave life to people in his own image. Creations made by people through childbirth cannot soothe even one painful memory that they hide deep in their hearts, because they have no life, but my world and my skies turn yellow thinking about why people place so much importance only on this.

(March 10, 2013)

# 언덕

봄이 오면
양지바른 곳에 물기를 먹은 새싹은 사뭇 꿈속에서 졸고
사랑하는 이의 가슴처럼 부풀어진 그리움
세월에 쫓겨 순결한 마음은 어느덧 흩어져 버린 하얀 구름
차라리 먹구름 되었으면 비라도 내리련만
도란도란 꽃피우던 행복한 언덕에 파아란 추억은 지울 수 없다

언덕에 올라 내려다보면 사람들이 지나간 길이 보인다.
능선 따라 자란 숲은 끝없이 방황하는 자의 쉼터이런가.
얽히고설킨 한 많은 사연을 부둥켜안고 밤새 바람과 더불어 이야기한다.
계곡에서 흐르는 물소리의 신음이 잦아들고, 부연 안개가 피어오르면
돌아서 가야 할 길 끝자락에 초췌하게 흐느끼는 이별이 보인다.

# Hill

When spring comes
shoots that drank water in a sunny place sometimes doze off in dreams,
and the longing that inflates, like the breast of that whom one loves.
The innocent heart chased away by time is now scattered into a white cloud.
If it was a dark cloud, at least it could rain,
but the pleasantly blue memories on the happy hill covered with flowers cannot be erased.

From on top of the hill, you can see the path that people passed.
The forest that grows along the ridges may be the resting place of those who wander endlessly.
Embracing the tangled stories, they speak together with the winds all night long.
When the moans of water flowing through the valley quiets, and a white fog rises,
you can see the sobbing farewell at the end of the path that they must return to.

다시는 편안히 쉬어갈 언덕을 찾을 수 없어도
내 뒤를 따라 이곳으로 오는 자가 또 있으니
이제 자리를 털고 일어나 가야겠다.
길 위에 널 부르진 자갈돌에 발바닥이 부르트며 상할지라도
한 걸음 한 걸음 무거운 발길을 옮기고 있다.

(2013년 4월 19일)

Though a hill in which one can find comfort cannot be found again,
  there is another person who will follow in my footsteps
  so I should not get up and leave.
  Even if my foot will be blistered by the gravel on the path,
  I take one step...after every other heavy step.

(April 19, 2013)

# 만우절萬愚節

만우절에
나는 아버지의 뒷모습을 보았다.
쓰던 일기장을 끝내지 못한 채 서투른 마침표를 찍은 아버지.
연이어 일기를 써주길 바랐지만, 나는 다시 쓸 수가 없었다. 삶의 장르 달라서 종이만 낭비할 것이 뻔 한 일인데
차라리 하얀 거짓말로 마침표를 찍었다면 온전한 마무리를 위해 맨손이라도 함께 썼을지도 모를 것을……

사월의 문을 열면
연둣빛 들판에 꽃길이 천상까지 뻗쳐 있어 나의 슬픈 카펫을 깔아드리고 싶다.
저승사자가 함께 가자 해도
차라리 하얀 거짓말로
곤충이나 동물들의 의태적擬態的 행동을 하셨다면 이토록 한恨이 되진 않았을 것을

만우절이 되면
마음속에 쓰고 있는 일기장에 아직도 나 홀로 마침표를 찍지 못한다.

(2013년 4월 20일)

# April Fool's Day

On April Fool's Day,
I saw my father's back.
My father was unable to finish what he was writing in his diary and was hurried to jot down his period.
He wanted me to continue to write his diary, but I could not. The genre of our lives was different, so it was obvious that it would only lay waste to paper.
If he had written his period with a white lie, I might have been able to write down a perfect ending with my bare hands...

When the gates to April open,
because the flowery paths reach out to the heavens on a green field, I want to lay my sad carpet for him.
Even if the Grim Reaper invites me,
if he had used white lies
and imitated the behavior of insects or animals, I would not be so heart-broken.

When it is April Fool's Day,
Alone, I still am unable to write my period, in the diary I write in my heart.

(April 20, 2013)

# 소금 기둥

 기름진 땅과 환락이 춤을 추기 시작한다.
 두 구멍을 통해 굴절해 들어오는 쾌락에 온몸은 전율을 느낀다. 땅은 지치기 시작한다. 이 모텔 저 모텔에서 잃어버린 젊음에 불꽃을 당긴다.
 한쪽 짓무른 구멍 언저리에는 헤르페스가 번져 추醜한 모양을 만들기도 하고 때로는 뇌 신경에 숨어서 면역체계가 무너지기를 호시탐탐 노리고 있다. 학업도 그만두고 과거의 숨소리가 묻어 있는 액세서리도 처분하고 고급 승용차를 타고 즐기기에 바빠진다. 썩을 대로 썩어버린 과거를 뒤돌아보지 말고 탈출하라고 신神은 명령한다.
 차라리 구멍 한 개로 세상을 보는 게 나을지 모른다. 신뢰도 팽개치고 도망갈 준비를 끝낸다. 고통이 와도 인내로서 미래로 가야 하는데 쾌락에 길들어진 습성을 버릴 수 없어 뒤를 돌아보는 여인. 영원히 사랑하겠다는 언약보다 가끔 분방奔放했던 과거가 그립다. 뜨거운 태양 아래서도 수족냉증에 걸려 혈액순환이 잘되지 않는다. 염병할 소금 기둥.

(2013년 4월 22일)

# Salt Pillar

Fertile land and pleasure begin dancing.

Pleasure that comes in refracted through two holes, makes the entire body shiver. The land becomes tired. Sparks are made to the youth lost in this motel and that.

On the edge of one hole festered with herpes spread to make ugly, and sometimes it hides in the brain nerves to wait for the immune system to crumble. The lady quits school, sell her accessories filled with memories of the past, and spend her time busily finding pleasure, riding a luxury automobile. God commands her not to look back at her rotten past and to escape.

It may have been better to look at the world with just one hole. Trust is cast away and preparations for the runaway are complete. Even if pain comes, one must be patient and go to the future, but the woman is unable to cast away her habits of pleasure and looks back. Instead of her vow to love forever, she misses her free-spirited past. Even under the hot sun, blood does not circulate due to cold hands and feet. Damn salt pillars.

(April 22, 2013)

# 해변을 걸으며

밀려오는 물결에 흔적 없이 사라진
두 쌍의 발자국
잡은 손 놓아버린 쓰라린 마음은 하얀 모래 빛
잊으려는 마음이 고통스러워 갈매기 끼룩끼룩 울면서 난다.

찰랑대는 물결이 밀물로 왔다가 썰물로 나간 것뿐인데
그렇게도 애타게 사랑했던 흔적은 순간에 사라지고
깨끗한 해변의 모래는 새롭다
여태껏 수 없이 짓밟혔던 해변은 얼마나 시원할까

해변의 파도는
쓰라린 사연들을 지우고 또 지우지만
끊임없이 만드는 철부지 인생

오늘도
외로운 발자국을 남기며 모래 위를 걷는다.

(2013년 4월 25일)

# Walking along the Seashore

In the onslaught of waves,
two sets of footsteps vanished.
The broken heart that let go of a hand that it once held is the white sand,
the painful attempt to forget comes in the cries of the seagulls.

The lapping water comes in withthe rising tide and goes out with the ebbs.
But traces of such burning love vanished in an instant,
and the sand of the clean beach is new.
I wonder how cool the beach that I stepped in so many times will be.

The waves at the seashore
erase painful pasts again and again,
but this child-like life makes them again and again.

Today again,
I walk on the sand leaving lonely footprints.

(April 25, 2013)

# 소나기 지난 후

 수억 년 강들이 강물을 실어 날라도, 폭우가 홍수 되어 바다로 흘러도 바다를 다 채우지 못합니다. 자연의 섭리를 풀기는 아직 인간이 너무 약하기 짝이 없습니다.
 파도처럼 밀려오는 잡다한 언어가운데 잘못 새어 나온 말은 하필이면 상처의 흔적만 남기게 됩니다. 이럴 때 마음속에 숨어 있던 자존심까지 동원하여 서로가 키워가던 부푼 풍선조차 소리 없이 꺼지게 합니다. 언어의 자궁에서 생산할 유순하고 아름다운 언어는 기능 다한 월경처럼 멎어 버립니다. 너 아니면 어디 없나, 잘 해보라지. 자신 있게 하던 말이 시간이 지날수록 허물어지고 마음속에는 미움과 사랑이 서로 교차하며 심히 우울하게 됩니다. 밖에서 귀에 넣어 주는 언어는 쉴 새 없이 불 지르는 말만 찾아서 들려줍니다. 정신이 혼미하여 과거가 잊혀지고 상대조차 사람으로 보이지 않습니다. 때마침 비조차 세게 내립니다. 어두운 밤이 왔습니다. 밤이 너무 깁니다. 그렇지만 모든 것은 정체되어 있기만 하는 것은 아닙니다. 아침이 되자 다시 비가 퍼붓습니다.
 만일 빗방울이 쏟아질 때 스트레스를 풀 수 있다면, 미움과 좌절의 마음을 다 모아, 폭우에 내 놓아 깨끗이 씻어보세요. 고뇌의 쓰나미가 쓸고 간 자리, 절망의 언덕에서 잠시 머물게 되면, 푸른 하늘의 구름 같은 후회만 떠 있음을 알게

# After the Shower

Even if billions of years old rivers carry waters, and even if heavy rains become floods and flow into the seas, the seas can never be full. Humans are too minuscule to solve the providence of nature.

Of the many languages that crash in like waves, sometimes they only leave traces of wounds. At such times, the pride hidden in one's heart is employed to quietly deflate the balloons that were inflated together. Beautiful and gentle language that should be produced in the womb of nature stops like menstruations that are no longer functional. There's plenty of other options than you. Such confidence crumbles with the passage of time and as love and hatred cross paths, it becomes very depressing. Language that is placed in the ear from the outside only, contain words that will fuel the fire. One loses consciousness and forgets the past, and the other person does not even look human. Then, strong rain falls. The dark night has fallen. The night is too long. But, not everything is stopped in place. Come morning, the rain starts again.

If you can relieve your stress whenever the rain falls, gather the hate and despair in your heart and place it under the torrential rains to clean it away. If you can stay a moment in the hill of despair where

됩니다. 이제, 너절한 변명의 옷을 벗고, 밭에서 새순이 자라나게 다시 북을 돋우고, 거름도 넣어야 하겠습니다.

 채워도 채울 수 없는 욕망의 바다 그 속을 헤매어도, 내 모습 이대로 온통 당신 생각으로 가득한 내 영혼.
 시련이 지난 후 함께 걷는 걸음에는 하늘빛 고요히 푸르러 갑니다.

(2013년 4월 28일)

the tsunami and anguish washed away, you will notice only regret, like a cloud in the blue skies that remains. Now, take off your clothes of shabby excuses, play the drums that make new shoots grow in the field, and also fertilize the ground.

Even if I wander in the seas of desire that can never be filled, my soul is always filled with thoughts of you.

After the tribulations, in the path we walk together, the skies quietly become bluer.

(April 28, 2013)

# 태종대

태고의 풍광을 즐기려
신선神仙이 공룡을 타고 내려와 놀던 곳

여기에
태종 무열왕은
삼국통일의 기쁨을 감출 길 없어
화살로 바람을 갈랐고
야망을 구름 위로 띄우던
그때의 정기가 아직 흐르고 있음이라

안고 싶어도 안지 못한
오륙도*를 바라보며 휘돌아 가면
기암절벽에 생명줄 놓지 않고
나란히 서 있는 소나무들
안개도 아찔하여 맴돌다 간다

고된 걸음 걸어가는 구비길 따라
멈추어 버린 숱한 삶
절벽에 서려 있어
바람도 울고 파도조차 울어

# Taejongdae

Place to enjoy the scenery of ancient time
Where taoists came and played by riding down dinosaurs

King Taejong Muyeol
With unbridled joy at the union of three kingdoms
Divided the wind with an arrow
And set ambition above the clouds
That energy still flows here

Pine trees standing side by side
Grasping their lifelines along rugged precipices
Along a curve facing Oryuk-Island
That can't be hugged in spite of the desire to hug
And even fogs feel dizzy, linger around and leave

Many lives have stopped
Along the curved, hard-beaten paths
Still misted on the clift
The wind and waves cried
Beyond the mother-son status

모자상母子像 너머엔
포말로 하얗게 부서지는 애달픈 사연

한쪽 다리 빠져가며 물 위를 걷는
베드로**가 되어
슬픔도 기쁨도 함께 가진 태종대
역사의 바다 위를 걸어서 간다.



*오륙도: 부산광역시 남구 용호동에 있는 섬. 바라보는 방향에 따라 다섯 개 또는 여섯 개로 보이기 때문에 이렇게 이른다. 면적은 0.02㎢. 명승 제24호
**베드로: 예수의 제자(마태복음 14장 30~31절)

Sad stories break in white bubbles

Like Peter
Who sank into the water as he walked
Walk on the Taejongdae sea
With a history of both sorrow and joy

*Oryuk-Island: Situated in Yongho-dong, Nam-gu, Busan. It received its name because it looks like five and sometimes six islands depending on the direction. Area 0.02$km^2$, scenic spot #24
*Peter: One of the disciples of Jesus (Matthew 14:30-31)

# 나이아가라 폭포에서

몇 번이나 와도
또다시 보고 싶어
돌아온 방랑자

혈류병 앓던 여인처럼
자연의 신비가 스며있는
그의 옷자락을 만져본다

태초와 현실에 무지개 얹어놓고
노아의 홍수 한 줄기를
이곳으로 돌린 듯

천둥과 같은 폭포소리로 위엄을,
물보라로 그의 영광을
나타냄이라

은혜처럼 떨어진 폭포수는
고요한 강물 되어 흐르는데
나는 강섶에 던져진 모난 돌

# Niagara Falls

After several visits
The rover came back
To see it again

Like the sick woman
Who touched His hem
Infiltrated by the mystery of nature

As if the rainbow was placed on the beginning of the world and reality
And one stream of Noah's flood
Is placed in here

The thunderous roar
Shows His dignity
And the spray radiates his glory

Pouring down like blessings
It becomes a quiet river
Running around my rough edges

정처 없는 삶도 녹아드는
이 강물에
나는 깎이고 깎여 작은 몽돌이 된다.

(2011년 6월 1일)

My edges become rounded
Soothed by the river
Where even roaming lives can find peace

(June 1, 2011)

# 몽돌

나 다시 태어나면 작은 몽돌 되련다.
세파에 부딪혀 모난 쪽이 깎기고
파도에 채여서 해변까지 굴러 와도
표정 하나 변함없고,
푸른 물이 베여와도 제 색깔을 간직하는
하얀 몽돌
티 하나 볼 수 없는 깨끗한 얼굴이
어쩌면 이렇게 예쁘게 보일까
누구한테 배웠는지
억겁의 세월 동안 참아온 인내
어디에다 쓰이려고 이런지 모르지만
나 다시 태어나면 하얀 몽돌 되련다.

(2011년 6월 2일)

# A Round Rock

Oh, to be reborn as a small round rock
White; with edges rounded by hardships
With unchanging expressions
Even when tossed and beaten by waves
Unstainable by the blue water
With a pretty and clean face
Unblemished by dust
Possessing patience
In the face of eternity
Oh, to be reborn as a white small round rock

(June 2, 2011)

# 이기대 산책

아내가 사준 흰 운동화 신고 이기대에 산책하면
해변의 계단은 파도소리 젖어 있어
출렁이는 파도 따라 일렁이는 구름다리
장난기가 발동하여 쿵쿵 걸음 걸으면
중심 잃는 아낙네의 겁 많은 웃음소리
내가 걷는 해변에 새소리 벌레 소리 파도와 어우르면
조용한 아침에 물에 젖은 붉은 해가 바다를 달구며
커다랗게 떠오르고 있다.
산책로를 따라서 돌아 오면은
내가 사는 아파트에 사람들이 분비고
바쁘게 하루가 시작되는데
나는 어찌 물든 저녁놀이 왜 그리 그리울까?

(2011년 6월 2일)

## Walking at Yigidae

As I walk at Yigidae wearing white tennis shoes purchased by my wife
   The stairs to the beach were wet
   I stepped onto the overpass, which swayed with the rolling waves
   Stumbling women shrieked with fearful laughter
   And the birds and bugs sang a duet accompanied by the waves
   The wet red sun burned the sea
   Swelling as it rose into the air
   Walking back along the path
   To my crowded apartment
   Bustling with industrious activities
   I wonder why I miss that dyed sunset so much?

(June 2, 2011)

## 낙원의 끄트머리에서

선악과 따먹다 쫓겨난 인간들은
나뭇잎으로 아래를 가렸다
따먹은 입을 가려야 할 텐데…….
엮어 맨 가리개의 이파리 하나하나에는
절정에 다다르는 신음과 고통이 들어 있어
어둠을 맞이하기 위해서는
에너지를 공급할 탄소동화작용이 필요한 게다
그래서 먹음직한 과일의 색깔을 내는 모양이다

노을 뒤끝에 가을이 기다리고 섰다.
서쪽 하늘은 가리던 이파리를 물들게 하고
작가는 혼동의 펜으로 엮어 놓은 줄 위에 드라마를 쓰는데
이파리는 뚝뚝 떨어진다.
옛 에덴에서 길들여진 나체가 그리운 모양이다.
보다 못한 시꺼먼 구름은 밤을 싣고 와서 지표를 덮는데
빛마저 검게 물들어 버렸다
밤엔 별까지 야단이다.
가만히 있지 못하고 떨어지는가 하면
이미 사라져 없어도 반짝이며 지구의 동공에 들어온다.
비벼보지 못한 살갗이 타들어 가도

## At the End of Paradise

Exiled for eating from the Tree of Knowledge
They covered their bottoms with fig leaves
But they should have covered the mouths that they ate with…….
Because every leaf weaved and used to cover
Holds the groans and pains of reaching climax
So in order to meet the darkness
They may need carbon dioxide assimilation to supply the energy
Maybe that's why they are colored like fruit

Fall waits at the end of the sunset
The western sky dyes the covering leaves
An author writes a drama on strings woven with the pen of confusion
But the leaves fall down
Maybe they miss the nudity of the garden of Eden
A jet-black cloud loses patience and drags down the night to cover the ground
It dyes even the lights black
At night, the stars are in uproar
They can't stay still and fall down
And come in the pupil of the earth

밤의 신음을 느끼고 싶은 모양이다
아직까지 남아 있는 한 개의 이파리마저 파르르 떨며
가지에 붙어있던 그때를 그리워한다.


(2011년 6월 19일)

Twinkling as they disappear
Although the untouched skin gets burned
It may want to feel the groans of the night
One last leaf shivers and misses the time
When it could stay on the branch

(June 19, 2011)

# 징검다리

그리움 하나 갖다 놓고
발걸음 한번 재어보고

망설임 하나 갖다 놓고
뒤돌아보고

놓고
또 놓고

흐르는 세월 위에
내 마음 듬성듬성

보고픔이 물결에 씻기려나
애태우면서

은파 사이 건너가는
흔들리는 발걸음

(2011년 7월 5일)

## Stepping Stones

Put one longing
Measure the step

Put one hesitation
Look back

Put
Then, put again

My minds are here and there
On the flows of time

Worrying
That the longing will be washed away

Steps sway
Crossing the silvery moonlight

(July 5, 2011  02:05am)

# 자연自然의 신음呻吟

행복은 독 안에서 잠들고
불행은 무대에서 춤을 추리니
쓰레기로 버린 의식意識은
병들어 버린 어른들의 잠언箴言이라

저기 보아라.
양심을 버리는 저 군상群像들을!
대기大機는 니코틴을 흡입하고
물은 알코올에 중독된다.

썩지 않는 이기利己의 유산遺産은 지표地表에 떠돌고
수많은 세균과 질병만 삶의 터전을 갉아 먹는다

한 조각의 폐비닐이라도 긴 침묵沈默을 깨고 썩게 하든지
엽록소를 합성하여 자연自然을 숨 쉬게 하여
뿌연 공기만 들이키는 폐肺를
죽음의 공동空洞에서 구출救出하라.

# Groaning of Nature

Happiness is anesthetized by poison
Misfortune dances on a stage
Conscience thrown away like trash
This is the Proverb of sick adults

Look at those people
Who have thrown away their conscience
The atmosphere breathes nicotine
And water is addicted to alcohol

The never rotting heritage of selfishness
Floats above the earth
Multitudes of germs and diseases nibbling the base of life

Rescue the lungs that drink the misty air
From the hole of death
Let the plastic waste rot by breaking the long silence
Let nature breath by synthesis chlorophyll

암癌도
에이즈도
불치不治의 양심도
소독消毒하여 태워버릴 클린벤치가
우리의 뇌리腦裏에 그래도 살아 있기에

자연自然은 순수純粹 속에 생존경쟁이 있고
정직正直 속에 규율規律이 있어
아직, 삶의 근원根源이 사라지지 않았으니
펼쳐라,
그리고 읽어라!
자연自然의 경전經典을······.

(2011년 7월 24일)

A clean bench that can
Sanitize and burn
Cancer
AIDS
Incurable conscience
Is still alive in our brain

The nature is in struggle for existence in purity
And the rules are honest
The source of life has not disappeared
So
Unfold,
And Read!

(July 24, 2011)

# 바람 부는 날

세찬 바람에 잎들이 흔들린다.
가지가 굽고
둥지조차 흔들린다.

바람은 푸른 잎을 좀처럼 떨구지 못한다.

나무는 어릴 때부터
풍파風波를 피하는 방법을 가르쳤을 게다.
학교도,
학생도,
선생도 없이

오늘날 환경은 이렇게 좋은데
무너지는
스승과 제자의 자리

곤혹스런 세파世波를 비켜가는 방법을
나무에게 배울까
바람에게 배울까

(2011년 8월 8일)

# A Windy Day

Leaves sway
Branches bend
Nests swing

But the wind cannot make the green leaves fall

Even a sapling
Knows how to survive hardship
Without schools
Students
Or teachers

Today's environment is so nice
But the places for teachers and students
Have worn down

Learn from the trees
Learn from the wind
How to survive difficult hardships

(August 8, 2011)

# 신神이 쓴 책

황혼은 헤진 육신을 뜨거운 정열로 물들게 하지만
일몰은 불타는 태양을 잠재우는데
암흑 속으로 굴러가는 낙엽만은 쓸쓸하다

신이 쓴 위대한 책
게놈Genom*,
그 속에 운명의 유전자를
흩뿌렸건만

운명의 시계를 돌리는 대낮의 빛은
어둠에게 먹혀가는
삶의 유전자를 보고
조용히 울고 있다.

비록
뒤엉켜있는
삶의 혼미昏迷 속일지라도
각박한 탐욕의 덤불을 뒤지지 말자

# A Book by God

The dusk dyes the body with hot passion
But the sunset puts the burning sun to sleep
The dead leaves rolling in the dark feel lonely

The great book by God
Genom*,
The genes of destiny
Are dissected there

But the daylight that spins the destiny clock
Sobs quietly
Watching the genes of life
Being eaten by the dark

Although
Life is tangled
In chaos
Don't search the bush of heartless greed

피안彼岸의 거처居處 너머엔
내 사랑하는 자가 있을진저
외로움의 장막을 걷고
새로운 생명의 게놈을 펼쳐보니

환한 빛으로 오실 그대 향하여
사랑의 정열을 불사르고
슬픔이 없는 그곳에서
영원한 기쁨을 맛보리라

\*게놈(독일어: genom, 영어: genome 지놈): 유전체(遺傳體)는 한 개체의 유전자의 총 염기서열이며, 한 생물 종의 거의 완전한 유전 정보의 총합이다. 게놈은 보통 DNA에 저장되어 있다.

(2011년 7월 10일)

Beyond the dwelling of nirvana
My lover waits
Spread a new life genome
By rolling up the curtain of loneliness

The passion of love burns
Towards one who comes in bright light
To taste eternal joy
In the place where no sorrow exists

\* German: Genom, English: Genome: Dielectrics are the whole base sequence of a life; wherein lies the complete gene information of a species. The Genome is usually stored in DNA.

(July 10, 2011)

# 통영의 항구에서

청마의 깃발이
이충무공의 거북선에 꽂혀 휘날리는
항구는

밤새 바다를 싣고 온 파도
충렬의 뜨거운 피를
해변에 토했기 때문이라

작은 포구엔
비린내 섞인 질퍽한 삶이
문학의 아침을 여는데

펜의 잉크처럼 물든 김은
충효의 열정을 포옹抱擁했으니
충무김밥이 육지를 지키고 있음이라

내 사랑하는 자여
우리의 힘으로 함께 바다로 나가자
문예의 실로 엮은 충렬의 그물로 바다를 건지자

(2011년 5월 29일)

# At Tongyoung Harbor

The harbor
Where the blue horse banner
Waives from Admiral Lee's turtle

The tossing and turning waves
Spewed forth the Admiral's hot blood
Onto the sand

At the small port
The muddy life mixed with fish smells
Heralds the literary morning

The mist, dyed like pen ink
Struggled to embrace the Admiral's passion
So Admiral Gimbap protects the land

My dear let us go
To the sea with our strength
To scoop with the Admiral's net
Made with the threads literature

(May 29, 2011)

최원철 시집
# 산에도 들국화가 있더라

2013년 6월 10일 인쇄
2013년 6월 15일 발행
지은이 | 최원철
펴낸이 | 최장락
펴낸곳 | 도서출판 두손컴
　　　　부산광역시 부산진구 부전로 35, 301(부전동, 삼성빌딩)
　　　　전화 : (051)805-8002　팩스 : (051)805-8045
　　　　이메일 : doosoncomm@daum.net
출판등록 제329-1997-13호

ⓒ 최원철 2013 대한민국
값 10,000원
* 저자와 협의에 의해 인지를 생략합니다.

The Collection of Won Chul Choi's Poems
# Chrysanthemums in the Mountain

Printed on June 10, 2013
Published on June 15, 2013
Author | Choi, Won Chul
Publisher | Choi, Jang Rak
Publishing Co. | Doosoncomm Publishing Co.
　　　　　　　301 Samsung Bldg, 35, Bujeon-ro,
　　　　　　　Busanjin-gu, Busan, Korea (Postal Code : 614-850)
Telephone : 82-51-805-8002　Facsimile : 82-51-805-8045
E-mail : doosoncomm@daum.net
Registration No. : 329-1997-13

ⓒ Choi, Won Chul Korea 2013
Price : ₩10,000
* Damaged books are to be exchanged.

ISBN 978-89-97083-63-3-03810

「이 도서의 국립중앙도서관 출판시도서목록(CIP)은 서지정보유통지원시스템 홈페이지
(http://seoji.nl.go.kr)와 국가자료공동목록시스템(http://www.nl.go.kr/kolisnet)에서
이용하실 수 있습니다.(CIP제어번호: CIP2013007983)」